HINDU
Prayer and Worship

Rasamandala Das/Anita Ganeri

W
FRANKLIN WATTS
LONDON•SYDNEY

First published in 2006 by
Franklin Watts
338 Euston Road
London NW1 3BH

Franklin Watts Australia
Hachette Children's Books
Level 17/207 Kent Street
Sydney NSW 2000

Editor: Rachel Cooke
Design: Joelle Wheelwright
Picture research: Diana Morris

Acknowledgements: Radha Mohan Das: 11. J Davis/Eye Ubiquitous: 15. Dinodia: 13, 16, 21, 25, 27. Hutchison: front cover bl, 7. Pem Kapoor/World Religions Photo Library: 14. Glenda Kapsalis/ Photographers Direct: 23. Harish Luther/Ark Religion: 22. Michael MacIntyre/Hutchison: 18. Christine Osborne/Photographers Direct: 28. Christine Osborne/World Religions Photo Library: front cover r, 10, 29. Resource Foto/Ark Religion: 8. Reuters/Corbis: 5. Helene Rogers/Ark Religion: 19, 24. Claire Stout/World Religions Photo Library: 9, 12. Liba Taylor/Hutchison: 6. Isabella Tree/Hutchison: 26. World Religions Photo Library: 20.

Every attempt has been made to clear copyright. Should there be any inadvertent omission please apply to the publisher for rectification.

A CIP catalogue record for this book is available from the British Library.

Dewey Decimal Classification Number: 294.5

ISBN 0 7496 5937 8

Printed in China

Contents

Rasamandala Das is a practising member of the Chaitanya Vaishnava tradition of Hinduism, a devotional movement going back to fifteenth-century Bengal. He is the author of several books on Hinduism and holds an MA in Religious Education from Warwick University. Rasamandala selected these prayers to show the rich diversity of Hinduism, along with its everyday practicality, its enduring spirituality and its ability to speak to everyone, whatever their beliefs.

About Hinduism

Hindus are followers of a religion called Hinduism, perhaps the oldest living religion in the world. No one knows exactly when Hinduism began but it goes back at least 4,000 years to ancient India. Hinduism is a very varied religion with many ways of practising. Most Hindus, however, share the same basic beliefs.

Hindu beliefs

Many Hindus prefer to call their religion *sanatana dharma* which means 'eternal teaching'. They believe that this teaching applies to everyone, at all times and in all places. Hindus believe that beyond the material world we live in is something called Brahman (spirit). The material world is always changing and does not last but Brahman is unchanging and eternal. Brahman cannot be seen but is everywhere. Some Hindus call Brahman 'God'. Hindus believe in one

Om is a sacred sound. It represents Hinduism. It is pronounced 'A-u-m', and is chanted at the beginning and end of many Hindu prayers, and during meditation.

God but also in many deities who represent God's different forms and qualities (see page 11). You can find out more about Hindu beliefs throughout this book.

4

Hindus around the world

Today, there are about 1,000 million Hindus. Most still live in India where Hinduism began. But many have settled in other places, such as Europe, North America, Africa, the Caribbean and South-East Asia. There are more than half-a-million Hindus in Britain.

A Hindu procession in Kuala Lumpur, Malaysia. Hinduism has spread from India around the world.

Om. Oh Lord, the past, present and future universes are creations of your own powers. But you are much greater. This material world is only a quarter of the entire cosmos. The eternal spiritual sky makes up the remaining three-quarters.

About this prayer

This Hindu prayer comes from the Rig Veda, perhaps the oldest of the Hindu sacred texts. It is chanted in Sanskrit by priests during special ceremonies. The prayer expresses the Hindu belief that the material world we live in is repeatedly created, destroyed and recreated in an endless cycle. But, while the material world does not last, Brahman and the spiritual world are never-changing and have no beginning or end. It also expresses the idea that the spiritual world is bigger and more important than the material world.

Hindu Prayer and Worship

There are many different ways of worshipping in Hinduism. Most Hindus regularly visit the mandir (temple) to take part in puja, an Indian word which means 'worship' or 'giving honour'. Most Hindus also worship at home where they have a shrine.

Respectful greetings

When Hindus greet each other, they place the palms of their hands together and say 'Namaste'. It is an Indian word which means 'my respects to you, the soul within'. Saying 'Namaste' shows respect, not only to a person's physical, temporary body but to the real person, the atman (soul) living inside. Hindus believe that the atman is Brahman (eternal spirit) and is sacred, a part of God. Saying 'Namaste' shows that you see everyone as special, whoever they are.

Two Hindu women say 'Namaste' to each other.

Reciting prayers

When Hindus worship in the mandir, they sometimes place their hands together and recite prayers. Hindus believe that God lives in our hearts and is very close to us. Placing our hands together helps us to concentrate on God. Prayer helps people not only to speak but also to listen to God.

Hindu prayers

Many of the prayers used by Hindus today come from the Hindu sacred texts. The oldest are called the Vedas. The first Veda, called the Rig Veda, may have been composed over 3,000 years ago. The four Vedas include prayers, hymns and instructions for worship. Verses from the Vedas are used in many ceremonies marking important times in a Hindu's life, such as naming ceremonies, weddings and funerals. Other important and popular texts are the Ramayana (the story of Rama and Sita) and the Bhagavad Gita, which means 'the Song of the Lord'.

Sacred language

The earliest sacred texts were composed in the ancient Indian language of Sanskrit. Hindus consider it to be a sacred language spoken by the various gods and goddesses. Many Hindu prayers are still written in Sanskrit. In South India, Tamil is also thought to be a special language. Today, many prayers are recited in modern Indian languages, such as Hindi, Punjabi and Gujarati.

A woman reads from the Hindu sacred texts.

Worship in the Mandir

Many Hindus go to a mandir (temple) to worship. Generally, there are no set rules for when or how often they should visit. Hindus living near a mandir may go each morning to seek God's blessings before work or school. Families in Britain tend to visit mainly at weekends or on special days, such as festivals.

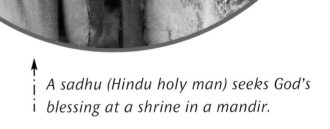

A sadhu (Hindu holy man) seeks God's blessing at a shrine in a mandir.

Inside the mandir

Hindus believe that the mandir is God's home on Earth. Each mandir is dedicated to one or more of the Hindu deities (see pages 10 and 11), or sometimes to a holy person. A murti (sacred image) of the deity stands in the main shrine. Hindus believe that God is present in the murti. Through the murti, God – who is actually invisible – accepts the love and devotion of the worshipper.

Worship in the mandir

On entering the mandir, worshippers take off their shoes as a sign of respect and to keep the mandir pure and clean. Then they enter the main shrine room, ringing a bell to announce their arrival. They stand in front of the shrine for a sight or viewing of the sacred images. This is called 'darshan'. With hands together and heads slightly bowed, they offer prayers and then leave a donation of fruit, rice, flowers or money. The flowers and money are used in worship. The food is used by the priest to prepare meals to offer to the deities. It then becomes prasad (sacred food) which is handed to worshippers as they leave the mandir.

A murti (sacred image) of Ganesh, the elephant-headed god.

O Lord Ganesh, with a curved trunk and large body, Shining with the brilliance of a million suns, Please take away all obstacles from my good actions.

About this prayer

This prayer is dedicated to Lord Ganesh, the deity who is shown with an elephant's head. Hindus believe that Ganesh removes obstacles and pray to him before starting puja or any new or important task. In a large mandir, there may be several shrines dedicated to different deities. Worshippers often approach them in a set order. It is usual to approach Ganesh's shrine first. It stands near the mandir entrance because Ganesh is the guardian of doorways and the lord of all beginnings.

Sacred Deities

After paying their respects to Ganesh, worshippers in the mandir say prayers to the other deities. Most mandirs have a main deity, or deities, standing in the central shrine. In smaller mandirs, there may not be a shrine to Ganesh. Worshippers go straight to the main shrine.

O Supreme Lord,
You are our mother,
father, brother
and friend.
You are the object
of knowledge
And our only treasure.
To us, you are everything.

About this prayer

This prayer is dedicated to Lord Rama, an earthly form of Lord Vishnu and a deity found in many mandirs (see opposite). Rama was born as a royal prince but his step-mother cheated him out of his kingdom and sent him into exile in the forest. Rama was married to Sita but the evil King Ravana kidnapped her. With the help of Hanuman, the monkey warrior, and his army, Rama fought and killed Ravana. He and Sita returned home to be crowned king and queen. Many Hindus believe Rama to be God himself.

Many different deities are carved on the gateway of this mandir.

Hindu deities

Despite the large number of deities in Hinduism, some are more popular than others or are thought to be more important. The main deities are Brahma, the creator; Vishnu, the protector; Shiva, the destroyer; and Shakti, the goddess (also called Durga, Kali or Parvati). Brahma is very rarely worshipped today but Vishnu, Shiva and Shakti have many followers. Two of the best-loved deities are Rama and Krishna who are earthly forms of Vishnu.

This shrine shows murtis of Rama (centre), his brother Lakshman (left), Sita (right) and Hanuman (kneeling).

I take shelter of Lord Rama's messenger, Hanuman,
Who is as swift as the mind, as powerful as the wind,
And in control of his mind and senses.
He is very intelligent, the commander of the army of forest creatures,
And the son of Vayu, god of the wind.

About this prayer

This prayer is dedicated to Hanuman, the monkey warrior and servant of Lord Rama. The story of Rama, Sita and Hanuman is told in the Ramayana, one of the holiest Hindu books. Hanuman is worshipped alongside Rama and Sita, and also on his own. Many sportspeople and soldiers pray to him for courage and strength. Hanuman is not worshipped as God but as a devotee of God.

The Arti Ceremony ॐ

The main ceremony held in most Hindu mandirs is called arti. In some mandirs, arti is performed five to six times a day, starting at around dawn and ending late in the evening.

Welcoming the deities

Arti is a ceremony used to welcome the murtis. The priest takes objects, such as lamps, incense, flowers and water. He waves each of them in a clockwise circle in front of the deities. He also rings a small bell. Worshippers then pass their hands over the lamp and respectfully touch their foreheads. The flowers are passed round and the water sprinkled over the worshippers' heads.

An arti ceremony takes place in a Hindu mandir.

Music in worship

During the arti ceremony, worshippers sing songs, called bhajans. Music is an important part of Hindu worship but it is not simply for entertainment. It is a way for worshippers to show their devotion to God. The songs are accompanied by musical instruments, such as tablas (drums), manjira (small hand-cymbals) and the harmonium. Sometimes, worshippers clap and dance along to the music.

↑ *Many Hindu songs celebrate the flute-playing deity, Krishna. He is shown here with his wife, Radha.*

Krishna sneaks out to
steal butter and yoghurt
Which he loves to eat.
Throughout the day,
he tends his cows
With his cowherd
friends.
Repeatedly, I offer
devotion
To the Supreme Lord.

About this prayer

The main bhajan during arti is dedicated to Hari (another name for Krishna), one of the best loved Hindu deities. The verse here is from another popular Krishna song. Krishna grew up in the village of Vrindavana in northern India and was brought up by a cowherd and his wife. As a child he was very mischievous and is well known for stealing butter and feeding it to the monkeys. Hindus also pray to Radha, Krishna's wife.

Mantras and Meditation

Meditation is an important part of Hindu worship. Meditating makes the mind calm and helps us to concentrate on one thing at a time. Hindus use meditation to see God, living within their hearts.

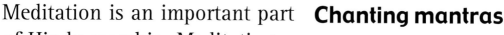

A sadhu sits cross-legged, meditating.

Chanting mantras

A mantra is a type of prayer which many Hindus use to help them meditate. It is a short group of sacred words or syllables. Usually the mantra is chanted over and over again to help people focus their minds. The mantra may be repeated silently or spoken quietly. Hindus often use a string of prayer beads to count off the number of mantras they have said. This practice is called japa which means 'whispering' or 'muttering'. Mantras are also chanted out loud to music.

Hare Krishna, Hare Krishna,
Krishna Krishna, Hare Hare,
Hare Rama, Hare Rama,
Rama Rama, Hare Rama

About this prayer

Many Hindus, especially worshippers of Lord Krishna and Lord Rama, use this well-known mantra. It is chanted both as japa (see opposite) and out loud to music. The word 'Hare' can mean Radha, Krishna's wife, or Hari, another name for Krishna.

Morning prayers

In Hinduism, there is no special day of the week for worship. The time of day is more important. The best time is around dawn, when our minds and surroundings are most peaceful. Many Hindus start the day by saying prayers or reciting a mantra. They may sit in front of their home shrine when the house is quiet and before they become too busy with their daily activities.

A Hindu priest recites the Gayatri Mantra in the morning by the River Ganges in India.

ॐ भूर्भुवः स्वः ।
तत्सवितुर्वरेण्यं ।
भर्गो देवस्य धीमहि ।
धियो यो नः प्रचोदयात् ॥

Om bhur bhuvah
svah tat
savitur varenyam bhargo
devasya dhimahi dhiyo
yo nah prachodayat.

I meditate on the
glory of the Sun
which, like God, is the
source of all life.
I pray that its divine
light will fill me
With hope and good
thoughts.

About this prayer

This prayer is called the Gayatri Mantra. It comes from the Rig Veda. At the top, the words of the mantra are written in Sanskrit; below that is how it is pronounced. Many Hindus repeat this mantra every morning. Some Hindus, especially priests, recite it three time a day – at dawn, midday and dusk.

Festival Prayers

Hindu festivals are important occasions for worship. There are hundreds of festivals throughout the year. Some celebrate events in the lives of the gods, goddesses or holy people. Others mark particular times of the year, for example the coming of spring. Many Hindus visit the mandir for puja, dance, music, drama and feasting.

Hindus celebrate Divali by lighting diva lamps in the mandir and at home.

Divali

In October or November, Hindus all over the world celebrate the festival of Divali. In India, Divali lasts for five days. Each day has its own customs and ceremonies. In countries such as Britain, Hindus often celebrate at the mandir over the nearest weekend. There are many reasons for celebrating Divali. Many Hindus remember the story of Rama and Sita (see page 10). They light tiny lamps, called divas, to celebrate Rama's triumphant return home.

Prayers for wealth

At this time, many Hindus also worship Lakshmi, the wife of Lord Vishnu.

Oh goddess Lakshmi!
You are the beautiful
temple of
Good fortune.
You represent the
fourteen gems
Of virtuous conduct.

Oh daughter of the
ocean of milk,
We pray to you
with gravity and
With affection.
Kindly shower upon us
Your blessings and
your wealth.

About this prayer

Most Hindu prayers praise God, or a particular deity, and then ask for something in return. This prayer is dedicated to the goddess, Lakshmi, the goddess of wealth and good luck. Lakshmi is especially worshipped at Divali. On the third day of the festival, Hindu business people hold a special puja in Lakshmi's honour. At this puja, they offer worship to pictures of Lakshmi and to their accounts' books in the hope of becoming more wealthy.

Navaratri

Another important autumn festival is called Navaratri (the festival of nine nights). It honours Shakti, who is also called Parvati, but often addressed simply as 'Devi' ('goddess') or 'Mataji' ('respected mother'). Other goddesses are also worshipped at this time, including Lakshmi, the goddess of wealth, and Saraswati, the goddess of learning. This festival is especially important to Hindu girls and women as it celebrates not only goddesses but women, nature and the ideal of being a caring mother.

↓ *Shakti (Parvati) with her husband, Shiva.*

Prayers for Liberation

Hinduism teaches that wealth and possessions do not last for ever. But everlasting happiness is possible. Many Hindu prayers are about seeking everlasting happiness through moksha, which means liberation or freedom.

Life and death

Hindus believe that, when we die, we are reborn in another body and so live on after death. This happens over and over again in the cycle of birth, death and rebirth. The quality of a person's next life depends on how they behave in this one. Good actions bring a higher rebirth. Bad actions bring a lower one. This idea is called 'the law of karma'.

The most important aim for Hindus is to achieve moksha, so setting themselves free from the cycle of birth and death.

From the temporary,
lead me to the eternal!
From darkness,
Lead me to light!
From death,
Lead me to ever-lasting life!

About this prayer

This prayer is from the Rig Veda (see page 7). It is often recited at public events, especially funerals. Hindus believe that death is the end of one chapter of life but the beginning of another. The purpose of life is to achieve freedom from the cycle of birth and death.

Prayers are said as part of puja in India to remember a loved one who has died.

Oh Lord Shiva,
you are not attached
to the pleasures of this world.
Seated in the Himalayas,
you are fixed in meditation.
Please grant me the power
to fix my mind on you
and thus gain liberation
from the endless cycle of birth
and death.

About this prayer

In addition to reciting formal prayers, many Hindus also make up their own. This prayer was written by a Hindu teenager. It is dedicated to Lord Shiva (see pages 11 and 17), who is often shown sitting cross-legged in meditation in the Himalayan mountains. Lord Shiva is an example of someone who is inwardly happy and does not seek pleasure through the senses and material possessions.

Giving up the world

In order to achieve moksha, some Hindus give up their homes and possessions. Even when they are young, they go to the forests or mountains to lead a simple life of prayer and meditation. Most Hindus, however, get married and try to enjoy the world. When they get older, they often retire and spend more time reading the sacred texts and making pilgrimages to sacred places. A few men leave home altogether to become sannyasis. A sannyasi is a wandering monk who gives up his belongings and family ties.

Hindu sannyasis, like this one, dress very simply – often in orange robes.

19

Prayers of Devotion ॐ

There are three main paths that Hindus may follow to reach moksha. Some follow the path of karma, or good actions. Others follow the path of jnana, or religious knowledge. However, the most popular path today is the path of bhakti, or loving devotion to God.

Loving devotion

For many Hindus in the past, their religion seemed strict and formal. Ordinary people felt left out because the priests did not allow them to read the sacred texts or, in some cases, enter temples. From about 1200 to 1700CE, a new type of Hinduism developed. Some great Indian saints taught about loving devotion to God, and the love that God gives in return. This was called bhakti. It quickly became popular, as teachers expressed their devotion through music and dance. They also wrote hundreds of poems, songs and prayers.

Followers of the Hindu saint Chaitanya (1486-1534) show their devotion to God through singing and dancing. Chaitanya was famous for chanting the Hare Krishna mantra (see page 15).

Love songs

One famous saint was Mirabai (1547-1614). She was born into a royal family and became a devotee of Lord Krishna. From an early age, she said that the only husband she wanted was Krishna. Eventually, though, Mirabai was married to a prince who treated her badly, and so she left the palace to lead the life of a wandering saint. She showed her love for Krishna through beautiful poems and songs. These are still sung and recited today.

An image of Mirabai with a vina (an Indian stringed instrument).

When the whole world is asleep, dear love,
I keep watch, parted from you.
In this beautiful palace, I sit alone and awake,
And see a forsaken girl,
With a garland of tears around her neck.
She passes the night, counting stars,
Counting the hours to happiness.

If I had known
That falling in love
Was to fall in with pain,
I would have beaten a drum,
Proclaiming far and wide
That love was banned for all.

About this prayer
This prayer was written in Hindi by Mirabai. It is written in the form of a love song. It shows Mirabai's great love for Lord Krishna and how painful it is to be parted from him. Many prayers, songs and poems have been written about this feeling of separation from God.

Childhood Prayers ॐ

For Hindus, the path to moksha and union with God is a long one. It may take many lifetimes. The one life we are living at the moment is just a single chapter in a very long adventure. Different stages in a Hindu's life are marked by special religious ceremonies. In these, prayer plays an important part.

Birth ceremonies

The ceremonies start even before a baby is born. When a Hindu woman is pregnant, she prays for the safe birth of her baby. Soon after the baby is born, the father places a drop of honey and butter on the baby's tongue. He whispers the name of God into the baby's ear and says prayers for his or her protection.

↓ *A Hindu baby's naming ceremony.*

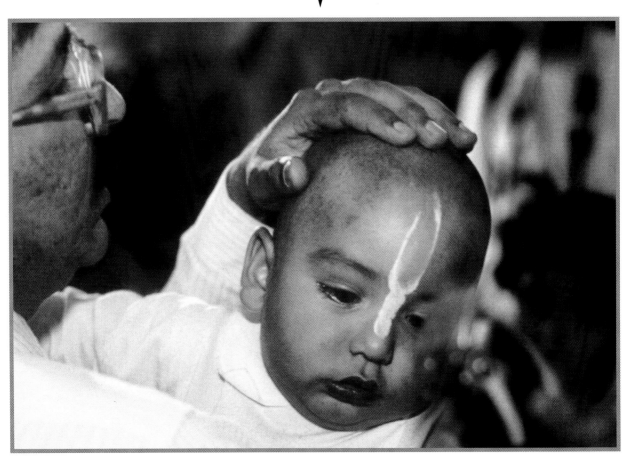

22

Oh my dear child,
May the moments deliver you
safely to the hour,
May the hours deliver you
safely to the day,
May the days deliver you
safely to the night,
May the days and nights deliver
you safely to the week.

May the weeks deliver you
safely to the fortnight,
May the two fortnights deliver
you safely to the month,
May the months deliver you
safely to the seasons,
May the seasons deliver you
safely to the year.
Oh my dear child,
may the years deliver you
safely to a long life.

About this prayer

This prayer is recited by the father or the priest at the baby's naming ceremony. It takes place when the baby is about 12 days old. The prayer expresses the hope that the baby will have a long and happy life. Traditionally, the family priests draws up a horoscope for the baby and, from the position of the moon within it, suggests a suitable name.

A Hindu boy with a sacred thread draped over his left shoulder.

Growing up

When some Hindu boys are about 10 years old, a special ceremony takes place. It marks the beginning of a boy's adult life. The boy is given a sacred thread which is draped over his left shoulder. The priest whispers the Gayatri Mantra (see page 15) into the boy's right ear. After that, the boy recites it silently or quietly to himself three times a day.

23

Getting Married

Most Hindus get married when they grow up. Their parents often help them to choose a suitable partner. Hinduism teaches that love does not happen automatically. Love and affection grow through respect, commitment and service to each other.

The wedding ceremony

A Hindu wedding is a complicated ceremony with many different rituals to be performed. During the ceremony, the bride and groom sit side by side and exchange flower garlands. A relative ties the bride's sari to the end of the bridegroom's shawl to show that they are joined together for life. The whole ceremony lasts for about three hours and is followed by giving gifts and blessings – and enjoying a great feast.

A Hindu bride in her beautiful wedding dress.

↑ *A couple walks round the sacred fire as part of their wedding ceremony.*

Seven steps

The ceremony takes place around a sacred fire. The priest chants mantras as the couple throws rice and barley into the flames. Hindus believe that God can accept offerings that are made in the fire. The couple walks round the fire, usually four times. Later, they take seven steps together. With each step, they make a vow, or promise, to each other. These vows are for food, good health, wealth, good fortune, children, happiness and life-long friendship.

Prayer by the bridegroom to his wife

'I am the sky, you are the earth.
I am the seed, you are the ground.
I am the mind, you are speech.
I am the song, and you are
the melody.'

Prayer by the bride

'I adore the Supreme Lord,
the unifier of hearts.
Now that I am leaving my parents'
home for my husband's,
I pray that God may keep us
together for ever.'

Prayer recited together

'Let us be devoted to each other.
Let us share each other's
joys and sorrows,
Wish each other well
And look upon each
other with love.
Let us live together for a
hundred autumns.'

About this prayer

During the wedding ceremony, the priest, bride and groom all recite prayers from sacred texts, such as the Vedas. These are normally in Sanskrit, but in Britain there is often an English translation. If the ceremony is at night, the groom points to the pole star. This, like the prayers above, show the important Hindus give to steadiness and commitment in marriage, based on love, respect, and valuing our differences.

25

In Daily Life

When people get married, life can become very busy. It is easy to think about work, money and holidays, and to forget about religious practices. Hindus try to spend some time every day, especially in the morning and evening, remembering God through prayer and worship.

Hindus bathe in the River Ganges.

Starting the day

Some Hindus chant the name of God as soon as they wake up. Then they take a bath or shower before they worship. In India, many people bathe in rivers. Certain rivers are believed to be holy so bathing in their water brings good luck and the grace of God. People also think that it helps them to achieve moksha (see page 18).

Within this water,
I call for the presence of sacred water
from the seven holy rivers:
the Ganges, Yamuna, Godavari,
Saraswati, Narmada, Sindhu and Kaveri.

About this prayer
This prayer includes the names of India's seven most sacred rivers. Hindus believe that reciting this verse makes ordinary water pure and holy. Some Hindus chant this prayer before taking a bath or shower. Priests also recite the prayer to purify water for washing items of worship, such as the bell and lamp. It is recited in Sanskrit.

Puja at home

Most Hindus set aside a room, or part of a room, at home as a shrine where they perform puja. This is usually a simpler version of the puja performed in a mandir. The shrine contains images of the family's favourite deity. These images may be murtis or framed photos or pictures.

A Hindu chants prayers before a meal.

If someone offers to me with devotion a leaf, or a flower, or a fruit, or even a drop of water, I will accept it because it was offered to me with love.

About this prayer

This prayer is a verse from the Bhagavad Gita, one of the most popular Hindu texts. It is often recited by Hindus before they eat a meal. It explains that, however small or unimportant something seems, it becomes precious if it is given with love.

Sacred food

Food plays an important part in Hindu worship. Food is offered to God, both at home and in the mandir. Small bowls of food are placed on a tray and put on the shrine, while prayers are recited. After the food has been offered to the deities, it becomes prasad, or sacred food. Many Hindus are vegetarians because they believe it is wrong to harm animals.

Prayers for the World

Some Hindu prayers ask God to help us enjoy the world. Other prayers are about freeing ourselves from the world and achieving moksha. There are also prayers that ask only for the chance to serve God, other people and all living creatures.

Oh Mother Earth, you
support people who speak
different languages
and follow different religions,
treating them all as residents
of the same house.
Like a cow that
always gives milk,
please make us prosperous
by pouring out a thousand
streams of treasure.

About this prayer

This prayer comes from the Vedas and is offered to the Earth, who is addressed as a goddess. The Earth is also compared to a cow, the symbol of motherhood, gentleness and contentment.

Gifts of the Earth

The Hindu sacred texts teach that wealth does not come from factories but from the natural products of the Earth. To show their gratitude for nature's gifts, Hindus offer prayers of thanks to God and to Mother Earth. Hinduism teaches that without respecting God's creation, a person cannot properly love God.

Hindu volunteers serve the needy with vegetarian food, helping both humans and the animals – all God's creatures.

Prayers for peace

i *Hindu children pray at home for world peace.*

Hinduism teaches that peace in the world is only possible if we are peaceful in ourselves. Prayer and worship are ways of achieving freedom from fear, anger, greed and unhappiness. A person must also give up the idea that the temporary body we have in this life is the real self. It is wrong to judge other people on whether their bodies are young, old, male, female, black or white. Inside we are none of these but the atman (the eternal soul).

I offer to the Supreme Being
My deeds, my words, my thoughts.
May everyone reach the Supreme Goal.
May everyone strive for the good of all.
May noble thoughts fill the minds of all.
May joy fill the hearts of all.
May selfish people become selfless.
May selfless people become wise.
May wise people go beyond death.
And may they help others
To enter the eternal world.

About this prayer

The ancient prayer above expresses the Hindu ideal that we are all eternal, sharing the same struggles and the same goal – to go beyond those struggles and reach God. Hindus believe this message is as relevant today as it has always been.

Glossary

Arti A ceremony of worship in which objects, such as lamps and incense, are offered to the sacred images to welcome the deities.

Atman The real person, or eternal soul, inside our temporary, physical bodies. Hindus believe that the atman is sacred because it is part of God.

Bhakti One of the three paths to moksha, 'bhakti' means loving devotion to God. It is a very popular type of Hinduism.

Brahman The spirit which is beyond the material world. Brahman is invisible, eternal, unchanging and present in everything. Some Hindus call Brahman 'God'.

Darshan A part of worship in which worshippers stand in front of the sacred images and say prayers and make offerings. The word darshan means 'sight' or 'viewing'.

Deities Another word for gods and goddesses.

Devotee Someone who dedicates their whole life to God.

Horoscope A chart drawn up for a Hindu baby. It shows the position of the stars, planets and moon at the time of the baby's birth.

Incense Sticks of sweet-smelling spices lit as part of worship.

Japa The quiet or silent repetition of a mantra as part of meditation.

Jnana One of the three paths to moksha, the word jnana (pronounced gyana) means 'religious knowledge' and 'knowledge of the way to approach God'.

Karma The word karma means 'action'. It refers to people's good or bad actions during this life which affect how they will be reborn. Good actions bring a higher rebirth; bad actions bring a lower one. Karma-yoga (performing good acts) is one of the three paths to moksha.

Mantra A short prayer or verse which is often repeated over and over again to help worshippers focus their minds.

Meditation A type of worship in which the person makes their mind calm and focused in order to concentrate on God living within our hearts.

Moksha Ultimate freedom or liberation from the continuous cycle of birth, death and rebirth.

Murti A sacred image of a deity that stands in the main mandir shrine and is the focus of worship. Hindus believe that God, who is invisible, is present in the murti.

Pilgrimages Journeys to sacred places, for example, rivers, mountains and lakes.

Prasad Sacred food. This is food that has been offered to the deities for their blessing, then shared out among the worshippers.

Puja The main Hindu form of worship in which worshippers make offerings to the deities. The word puja means 'giving honour' or 'respect'.

Sanatana dharma The eternal teaching or eternal law. This is the name that Hindus prefer to give to their beliefs, rather than the term Hinduism.

Sanskrit An ancient Indian language which is considered to be the sacred language of Hinduism. The earliest Hindu sacred texts were composed in Sanskrit.

Further information

Books to read
World Religions: Hinduism
Katherine Prior, Franklin Watts 1999

Sacred Texts: the Ramayana and other Hindu Texts
Anita Ganeri, Evans Brothers 2003

Keystones: Hindu Mandir
Anita Ganeri, A&C Black 2000

The Heart of Hinduism
Rasamandala Das, ISKCON Educational Services, 2002

Websites
www.hindunet.org
A general site packed with facts about every aspect of Hinduism.

www.indiancultureonline.com
Another useful site for general information about Hinduism.

www.worldprayers.org
A collection of prayers from many different faiths and traditions.

www.swaminarayan.org
The website of the fabulous Swami Narayan mandir in London, UK.

Index

32